ODD TIME STICKINGS

Contains: Compound Stickings for Odd-Meter Time Playing and Soloing

by Gary Chaffee

© 2013 Gary Chaffee
Exclusive Worldwide Distribution by Alfred Music
All Rights Reserved. Produced in USA.

ISBN-10: 0-7390-9668-0
ISBN-13: 978-0-7390-9668-0

T0043492

ABOUT THE AUTHOR

Credited with teaching some of the top players in the industry today, Gary has been earning the respect of musicians worldwide for over forty years. His list of students reads like a who's who of the contemporary drumming scene and his many books, including the highly popular four-volume *Patterns* series, as well as his two videos: *Phrasing and Motion* and *Sticking Time, Linear Time, Rhythm and Meter*, are considered a must for the serious drummer. This new book expands upon his unique concept of stickings by exploring their use in odd-meter situations. Students should find this material to be both challenging and rewarding.

ACKNOWLEDGEMENTS

Gary would like to thank the following people for there help in putting this book together: Steve Houghton and Jonathan Mover for reviewing the text, Dean Johnston for proofreading, John Weisiger for doing a great job with the manuscript, and Dave Black at Alfred Music for putting the whole thing together. Thanks guys.

Drumming...the next generation. Gary's grandsons, Tiernan and Finian O'Driscoll.

JOIN THE GARY CHAFFEE DRUM CLUB

Since odd-meter playing is such a big topic, I've decided to set up a Drum Club which will act as a kind of clearing house for ideas. Every student who purchases this book will be offered the opportunity to send in his or her ideas as it pertains to odd-time playing. These ideas will then be sent to all the other members of the club. Every month I will distribute the best ideas to all club members. This will hopefully generate a lot of creative input and will give you a chance to see what other people are thinking.

If all goes well, the Club will be expanded to include other issues related to the materials in my *Patterns* books.

The cost for joining the club will be $15 dollars per year and will entitle you to unlimited access to all the materials that are submitted each month.

To join the club, simply detach the form below and send it along with your check. Additional information concerning the club will be available on my website at garychaffee.com.

---detach here---

Name: _____   Address: _____

_____

Email: _____

Where did you purchase this book? _____

Send check or money order to: Gary Chaffee
16 White Oak Rd.
West Roxbury, MA 02132

Contents

Introduction

This book is an extension of the *Sticking Patterns* book I wrote some years ago. In this volume we're going to be exploring how these stickings could be used in a variety of odd meters. The use of different meters has become much more common in contemporary music, so it's important for students to understand how they work and what you can do with them. A number of sticking phrases will be shown for each meter. By working with these examples you will become familiar with many of the ways they can be organized. You can then use them to create your own time feel and solo ideas. For those of you who are already familiar with my sticking system, this should be very easy to do. If, on the other hand, you are new to my system, it won't take long to see how everything works.

MY STICKING SYSTEM

The sticking system I created consists of just 11 stickings, and is based upon how the singles and doubles are organized.

A STICKINGS (one single followed by doubles)

B STICKINGS (two singles followed by doubles)

C STICKINGS (three singles followed by doubles)

D STICKINGS (four singles followed by doubles)

E STICKINGS (five singles followed by doubles)

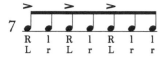

WHAT IS A STICKING?

A sticking is a sequence of right- and left-hand strokes that create a pattern. Most stickings are combinations of single and double strokes. When they are mixed together, they create a certain sound because of the motions our hands use to execute the singles and doubles (which are naturally different).

There used to be a concept that stated we should try and play everything flat, smooth and even. In other words, make our singles and doubles sound the same. This is silly because the sound of a sticking pattern is what gives it its unique character. We should embrace this, not fight it. Making all of our notes sound the same would be like a horn player playing everything staccato. (Just ask one of your horn or guitar playing friends how dumb that would be!)

There are a few instances when we do want to play things very evenly, as when playing double-stroke rolls. Most of the time, however, we want to allow a particular sticking to follow its natural shape because that's the musical thing to do.

ABOUT THE ACCENTS

You will notice that there are accent markings above the stickings. They are there for two reasons:

- Putting accents at these points will more clearly realize the shape of the sticking when you're playing both hands on a single sound, and

- they will help you identify the stickings when they are mixed together.

The accents are meant to be played slightly stronger than the other notes in the pattern. Just follow the natural motion the sticking suggests.

WHAT CAN A STICKING DO?

The **most important** thing you have to understand about stickings is that they are not rhythms. You can play any sticking in any rhythm and, when you do this, a lot of cool things can happen.

When you play a sticking in a matching rhythm (like a paradiddle in sixteenths), everything sounds straight up and down. But, when the sticking and rhythm don't match, you create a phrase because it takes a certain amount of time for the two to cycle. Here's an example using a three-note sticking in a four-note rhythm:

Now, what would happen if you used this same three-note sticking in a five-note rhythm?

Amazingly it works exactly the same. So, the number of notes in the sticking you're playing will equal the number of beats it will take to cycle the sticking **in any non-matching rhythm!**

"THIS IS THE FIRST LAW OF STICKINGS"

Now, what would happen in a situation where the sticking and the number of notes in the measure didn't match? Let's look at the same three-note sticking in 4/4 time:

It's still cycling every three beats, but now it also takes three measures for the entire phrase to cycle. And, believe it or not, this process works no matter what meter you're in!

"THIS IS THE SECOND LAW OF STICKINGS"

Even if you combine stickings (like a 4 and a 3), the sequence would take seven beats and/or seven measures. Just think for a minute about the possibilities this is going to offer you!

HOW CAN WE USE STICKINGS?

Time Feels—Stickings allow us to organize the notes in a time feel in endless ways. We can set them up to match certain things that are happening in the tune. We can also get the accents wherever we want, as they can really do a lot.

Soloing—Every sticking sequence you play will allow you to move around the set in a variety of ways. They also offer the potential of creating ideas of any length. The possibilities are endless.

When using stickings in either of these situations, the accents may change (or disappear completely) because now your breaking up the sticking between different sounds.

WHAT IS THE PURPOSE OF METER?

Meters are the structures we use to organize our musical ideas. Some meters have been around for a long time, and so they're typical structure is well known. Other, more exotic meters don't necessarily have a defined structure, and so we'll have a lot of options in terms of how we set them up.

ABOUT THE NOTATION

Owing to what we just talked about, there are many ways to approach different meters, and these can really affect notation. My wife is a classical pianist, and so I've looked at a lot of her music. The composers notate things according to how they want them to be played. They have two BIG advantages over us. The first is pitch, so when they set up a three-note sequence it's very easy to see. Secondly, they have articulation markings (symbols that represent how you're supposed to play the notes— staccato, legato, etc.), that are written into the notation. In a very real sense, stickings are our version of articulation since each sticking has a unique sound.

It's important to understand that our perception of a pattern is heavily influenced by what it looks like. For example:

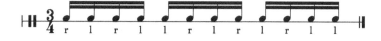

Many people would say this looks like a beat of singles leading right, followed by a beat of singles leading left, followed by a paradiddle. However, it's actually a combination of the 5C and 7E stickings. Let's add the accents to make it clearer.

Now you can begin to see the stickings, but it still needs something more. So, I decided to add brackets to make it absolutely clear what the pattern is.

This is the way I will be notating the examples when we're dealing with the more common meters. In situations where the meter doesn't have such a defined structure, the notation will be based upon the stickings being used.

Here's an example using the sticking sequence 5C/4B/4B in 13/16:

You will have different options in terms of how you perceive the pulse in such examples. This will be explained in more detail as the specific examples are explored.

PRACTICE PROCEDURES

Here's how you should practice the materials in this book. You have two primary goals. The first is to become really familiar with the meters, and all the different ways they can be organized. Secondly, you're looking for ideas that you can use for time feels, as well as solos.

GETTING TO KNOW THE PHRASES

Most of the examples in this book are set up as one-measure phrases. Each phrase is shown two ways: forwards (starting with the singles) and backwards (starting with the doubles). You should start by playing each example endlessly, as you're just trying to get into it, hearing it, seeing it, and feeling it. Do this with each phrase on the list.

As you're playing certain phrases, you may notice things that indicate some possible uses. Keep these ideas in mind because that's what you're going to be doing with the phrases once you complete the exercises.

APPLICATIONS

The whole purpose of this book is to take the phrases you're learning and use them to develop time feels and solo ideas. What I'm going to do is describe a general process you can use to develop such ideas. It will be up to you to come up with the specific versions on your own. You're going to have literally thousands of possibilities to work with, so you can have a lot of fun doing this and at the same time develop your own concepts about how you're going to approach odd-meter playing.

APPLICATION #1: TIME FEELS

It's very easy to use sticking phrases to set up time feels. Here's what you do.

Step 1—Pick the phrase you want to work with. (I'm going to use 3A/5A/4B in 3/4 time to demonstrate.)

Step 2—Decide on a basic accent line. (Note: As was mentioned previously, once you start using stickings in this situation, the accents can be put wherever you want them.)

Step 3—Try different bass drum lines. You will have many choices. Here's one possibility:

Once you get your basic idea in place, you will have many options in terms of how you can expand it. You can change the accent line. You can add a different bass drum line. Here's an example using both of these options to set up a two-measure phrase:

Another possibility would be to move some of the hand notes to other sounds on your set, as in the following example:

ABOUT THE ACCENTS

Technically speaking, accenting on single strokes is probably the easiest. However, accenting on the first or second note of a double stroke (as in the example above) is not that difficult, and is something you definitely want to learn how to do.

Not only does it give you more choices as to where you can put the accents, it also changes the 'sound' of the accents.

One other thing you want to consider when developing your accent lines is the possibility of bringing the right hand over from the hi-hat (or cymbal) to the snare drum. This will give you even more accent choices.

About the Bass Drum Lines

Ideally, it would be possible to develop the ability to place the bass drum notes anywhere within a pattern. This does take a certain degree of skill, especially given the fact that you're going to be working on hundreds of different phrases. My suggestion would be to work first with just a few phrases you really like. As you repeat a certain phrase over and over, you should notice that moving the bass drum around gradually becomes easier. This ability will continue to expand over time.

Application #2: Solo Ideas

Stickings are one of the most important tools we have in our arsenal. Each sticking offers unique ways of organizing the sounds on the set. However, given the wide variety of set ups drummers now use (anywhere from a standard 3 or 4 piece kit to leviathans of 10 or 20 or more toms, multiple snares, bass drums, endless numbers of cymbals, as well as lots of extra exotica and toys), it would be impossible to show examples for all of these. However, what I can do is discuss a kind of general approach you can use when learning to move stickings around the set.

As a practice format you may want to begin with a typical three measures of time, followed by a one- measure solo routine. Start by repeating this basic routine many times, playing the sticking phrase on the snare drum. Then, start working on the following:

Step 1—Work with the singles in one or both hands.

You can start by moving some or all of the singles in each hand separately at first.

Depending on how many there are (and how many sounds you have), certain possibilities will present themselves. Go with the obvious first. Then, experiment with moving some of the singles in both hands.

Step 2—Work with all the notes in one hand.

Try moving both the singles and doubles that are in one hand. Again, work with each hand separately at first, and then mix them.

ABOUT THE DOUBLE STROKES

It's also possible to move just the doubles to the various sounds on your set. Another great thing you can do is to break up the two notes between different sounds. If you go to my *Sticking Patterns* book (pgs.28-33) you will find a long set of exercises that will take you through all the moving and broken doubles possibilities. Please check these out thoroughly because they will give you a great deal of flexibility when working with the doubles in stickings.

As you work through these soloing routines, you'll begin to develop a great deal of flexibility with the stickings on the set. You will eventually get to the point where you can really be creative in how you use them, which is really the whole point.

EXAMINING PART II—ADDITIONAL POSSIBILITIES

In addition to the applications we've been discussing, there are a number of other possibilities that exist for these examples, such as mixing phrases together, incorporating different materials, using different rhythms, etc. There is no reason why you can't involve some of these ideas right from the very beginning of your work with this book. Therefore, I suggest you take a few minutes NOW to read through this section and become familiar with these issues.

Then, as you complete each set of exercises, you can experiment with some of these additional possibilities, as well as the basic routines that have been suggested.

Good luck and have fun!

Part I:
Meter Studies

Sticking Phrases in 3/4

I decided to start with 3/4 because it's a relatively common meter. The sixteenth notes are notated normally. Brackets are included to help clarify the stickings. Each example will be shown in the following two ways: leading with the singles (left column) and leading with the doubles (right column).

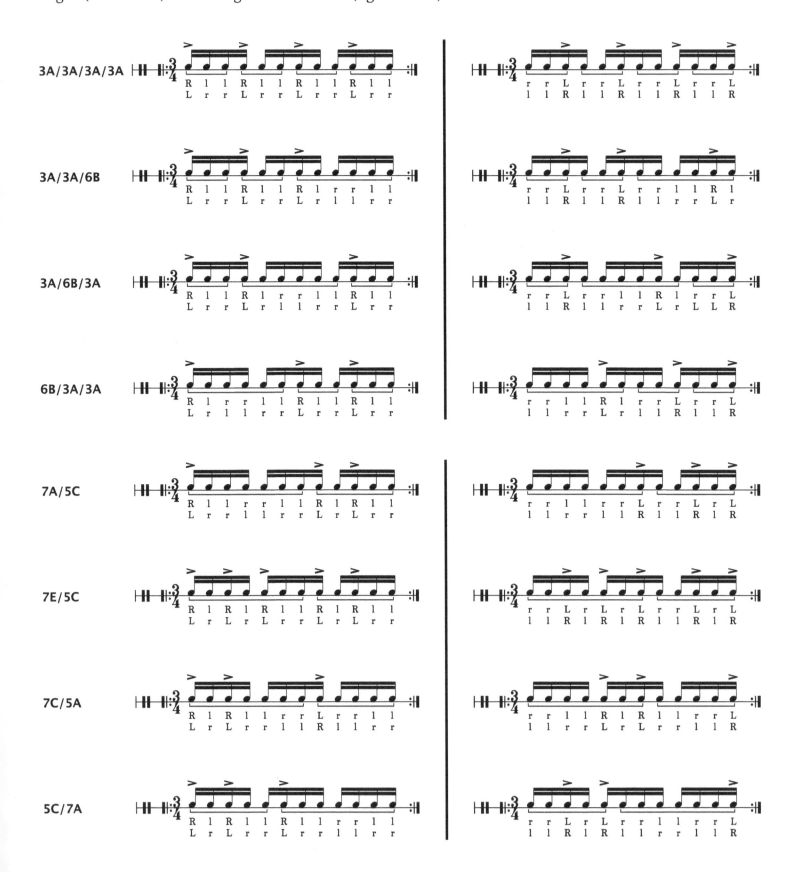

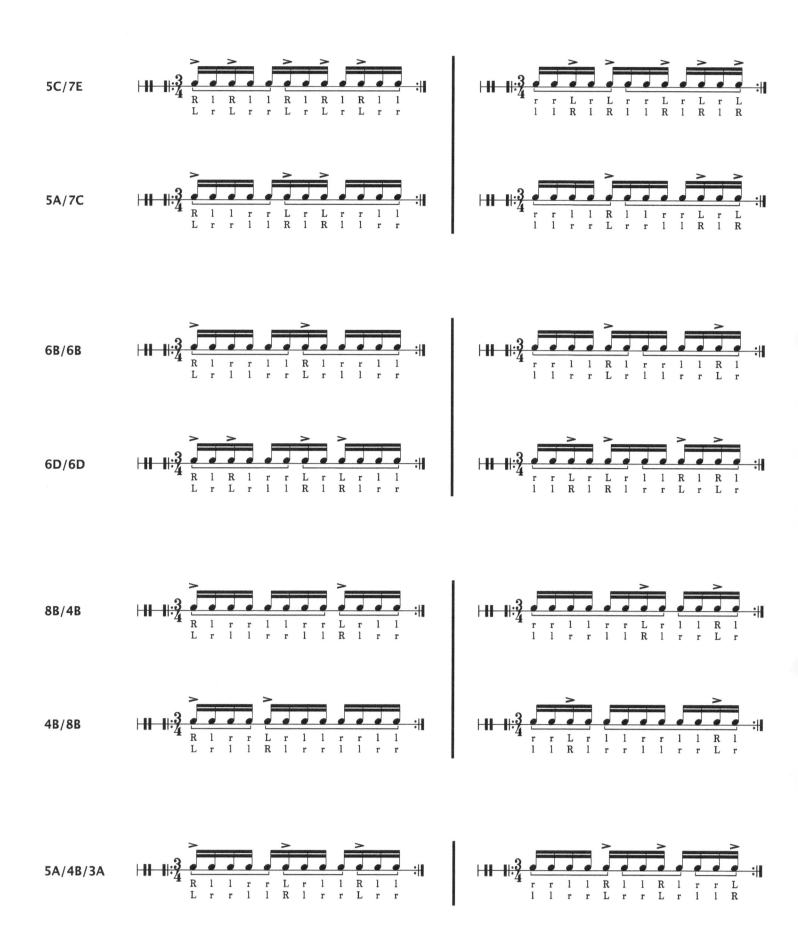

5A/3A/4B

```
R l l r r L r r L r l l
L r r l l R l l R l r r
```

```
r r l l R l l R l l R l
l l r r L r r L r r L r
```

4B/5A/3A

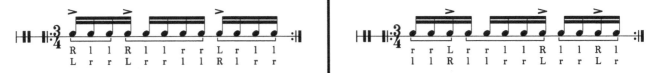

```
R l r r L r r l l R l l
L r l l R l l r r L r r
```

```
r r L r l l r r L r r L
l l R l r r l l R l l R
```

4B/3A/5A

```
R l r r L r r L r r l l
L r l l R l l R l l r r
```

```
r r L r l l R l l r r L
l l R l r r L r r l l R
```

3A/5A/4B

```
R l l R l l r r L r l l
L r r L r r l l R l r r
```

```
r r L r r l l R l l R l
l l R l l r r L r r L r
```

3A/4B/5A

```
R l l R l r r L r r l l
L r r L r l l R l l r r
```

```
r r L r r L r l l r r L
l l R l l R l r r l l R
```

Use this page to write out some original ideas in 3/4.

Use this page to write out some original ideas in 3/4.

Sticking Patterns in 5/8

The pulse for 5/8 is:

You may use the pulse above, or follow the groupings below.

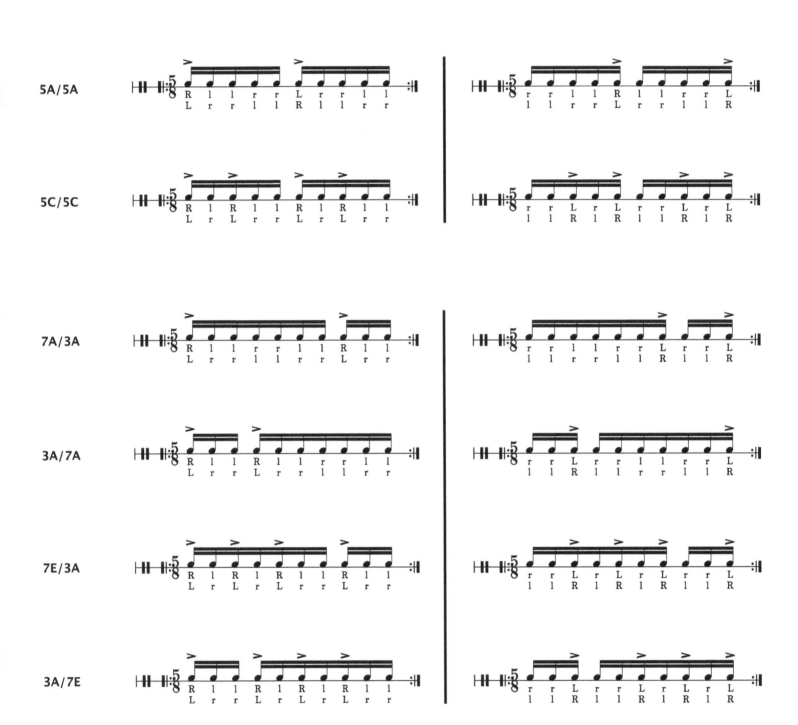

6D/4B

4B/6D

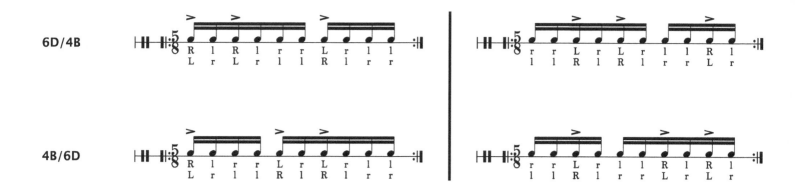

Use this space to write out some original ideas in 5/8.

Sticking Patterns in 11/8

This meter doesn't have a normal pulse. The notes will be grouped according to the stickings which will set up the pulse.

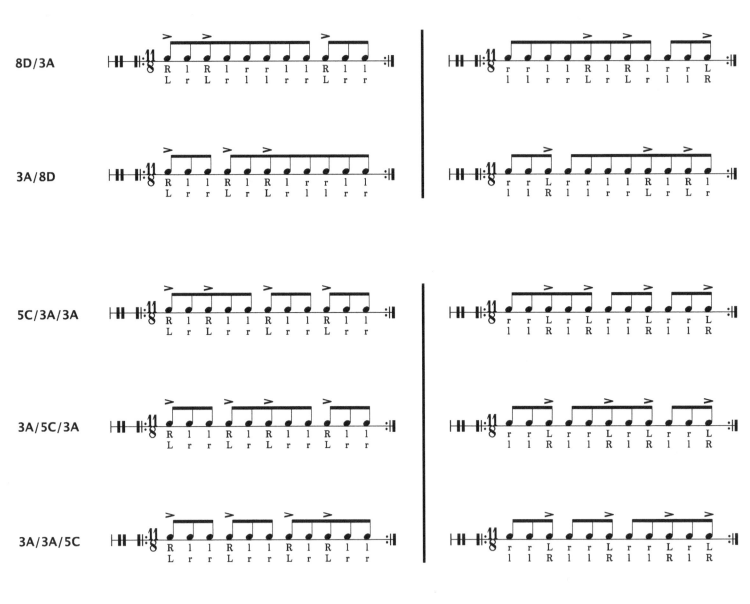

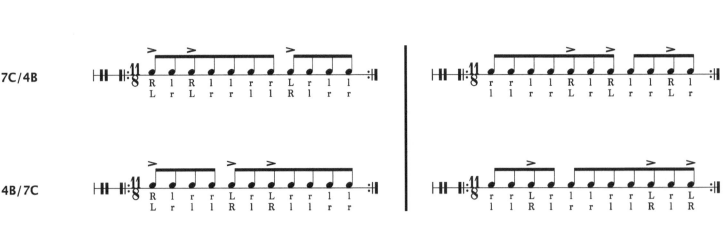

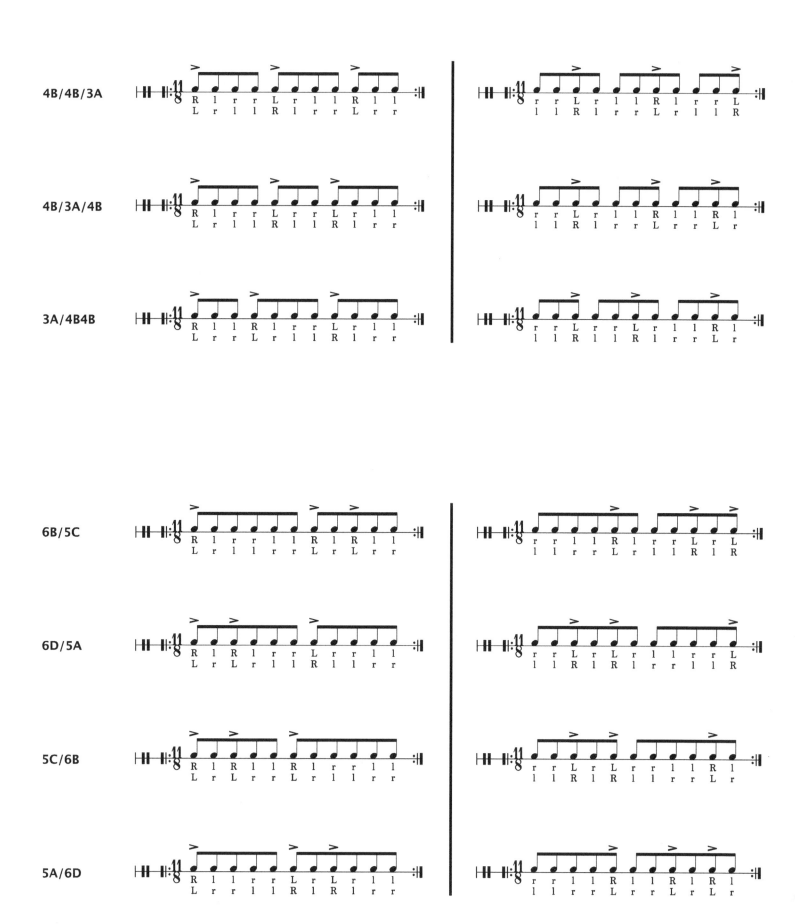

Use this page to write out some original ideas in 11/8.

Sticking Patterns in 13/16

Here is another meter that doesn't have a normal pulse. Therefore, the notes will be grouped according to the stickings, setting up an uneven pulse.

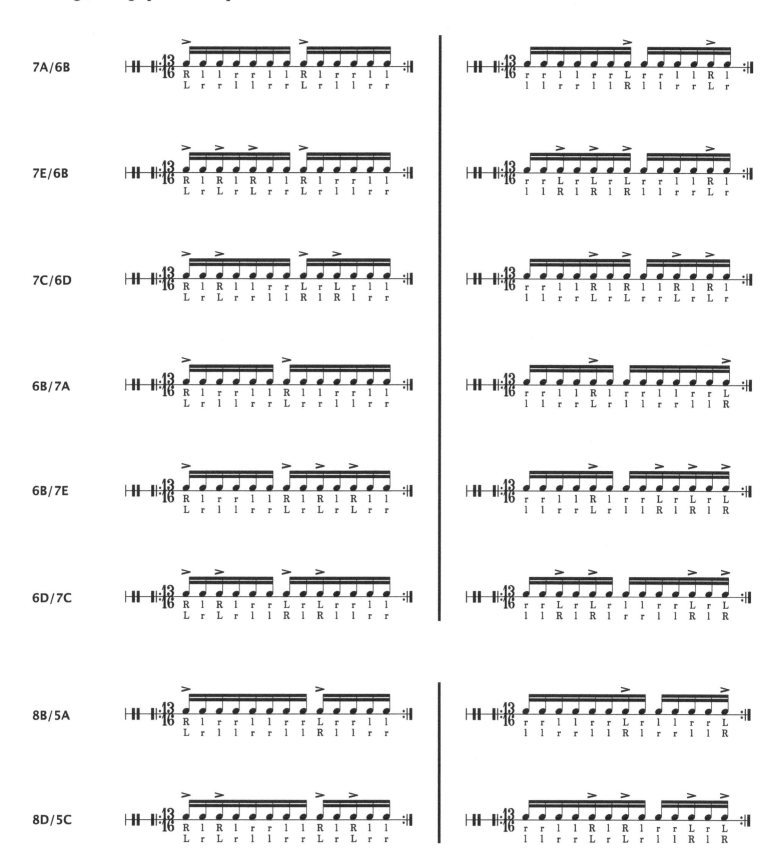

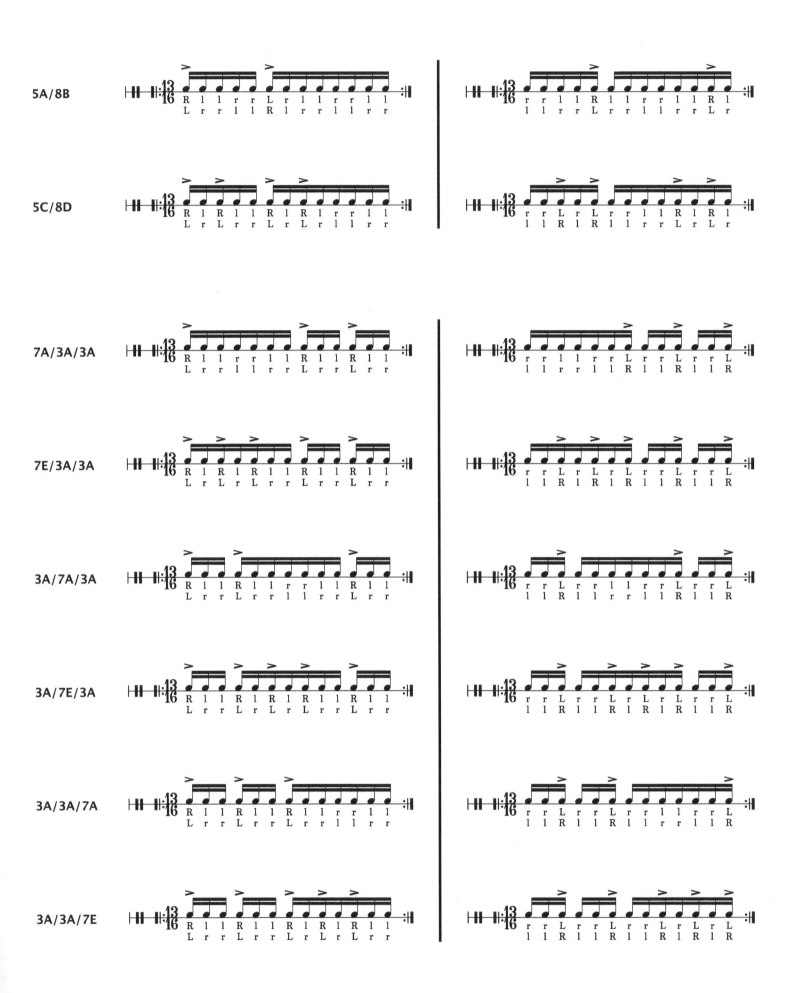

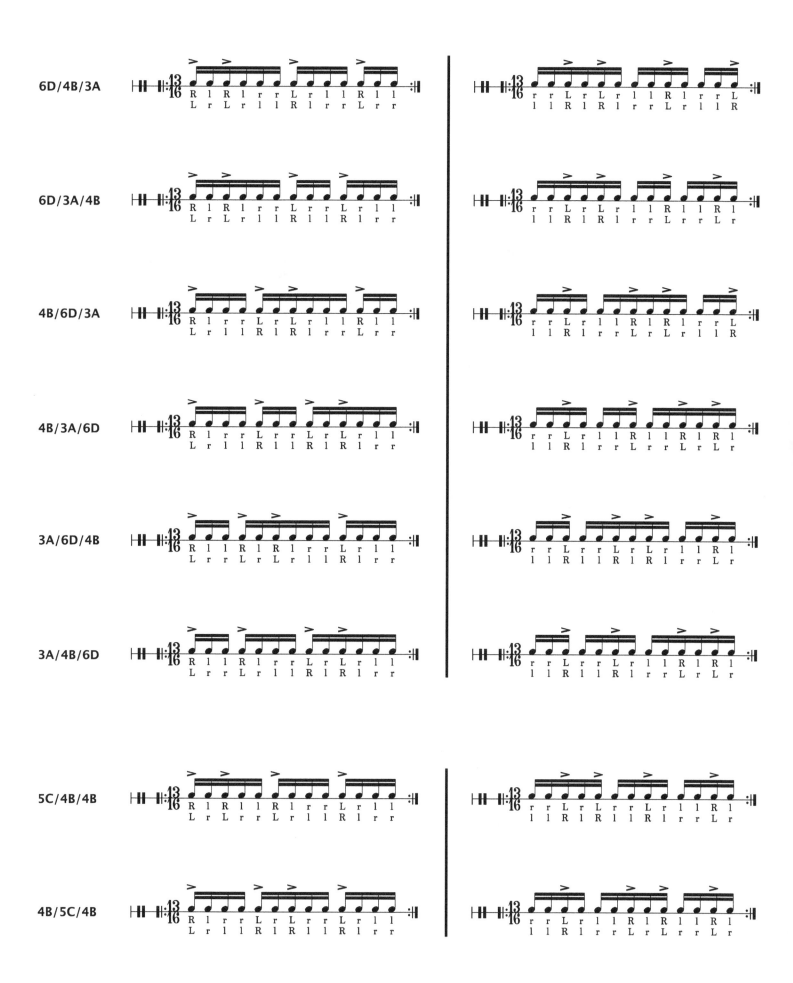

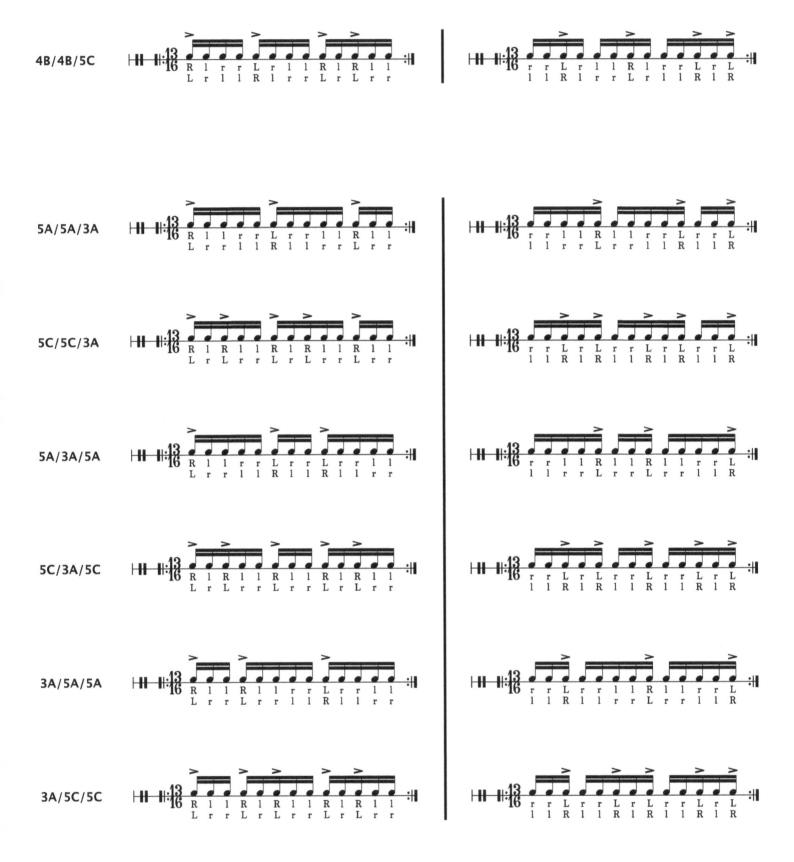

Use this page to write out some original ideas in 13/16.

Use this page to write out some original ideas in 13/16.

Sticking Patterns in 7/8

The pulse for 7/8 is:

You may tap the pulse above, or follow the groupings below.

7A/7A

R l l r r l l R l l r r l l
L r r l l r r L r r l l r r

r r l l r r L r r l l r r L
l l r r l l R l l r r l l R

7C/7C

R l R l l r r L r L r r l l
L r L r r l l R l R l l r r

r r l l R l R l l r r L r L
l l r r L r L r r l l R l R

7E/7E

R l R l R l l R l R l R l l
L r L r L r r L r L r L r r

r r L r L r L r r L r L r L
l l R l R l R l l R l R l R

7A/7E

R l l r r l l R l R l R l l
L r r l l r r L r L r L r r

r r l l r r L r L r L r L
l l r r l l R l R l R l R

7E/7A

R l R l R l l R l l r r l l
L r L r L r r L r r l l r r

r r L r L r L r r l l r r L
l l R l R l R l l r r l l R

8B/6D

R l r r l l r r L r L r l l
L r l l r r l l R l R l r r

r r l l r r L r l l R l R l
l l r r l l R l r r L r L r

8D/6B

R l R l r r l l R l r r l l
L r L r l l r r L r l l r r

r r l l R l R l r r l l R l
l l r r L r L r l l r r L r

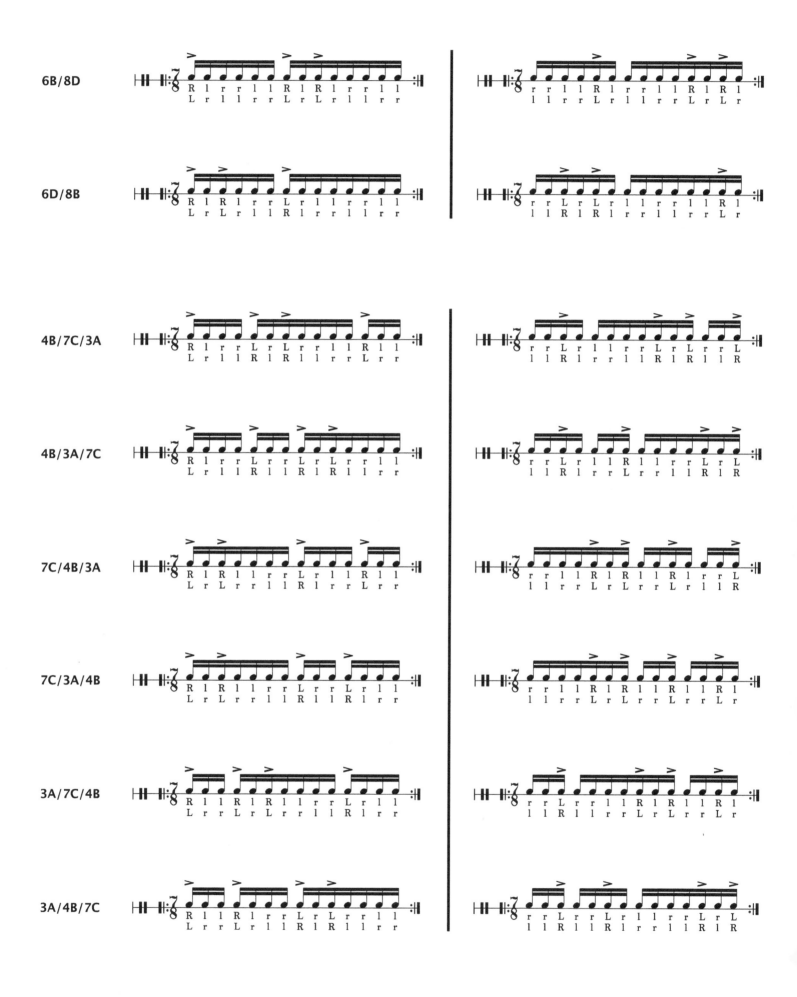

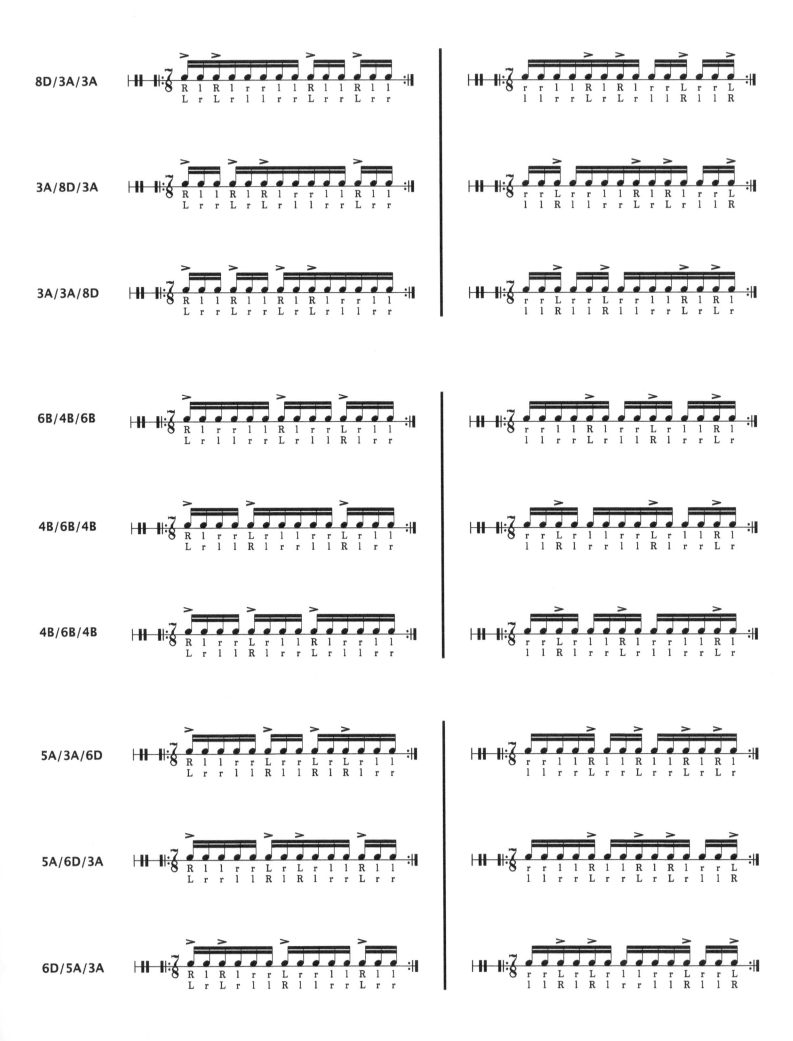

6D/3A/5A

3A/6D/5A

3A/5A/6D

6B/5C/3A

6B/3A/5C

5C/6B/3A

5C/3A/6B

3A/5C/6B

3A/6B/5C

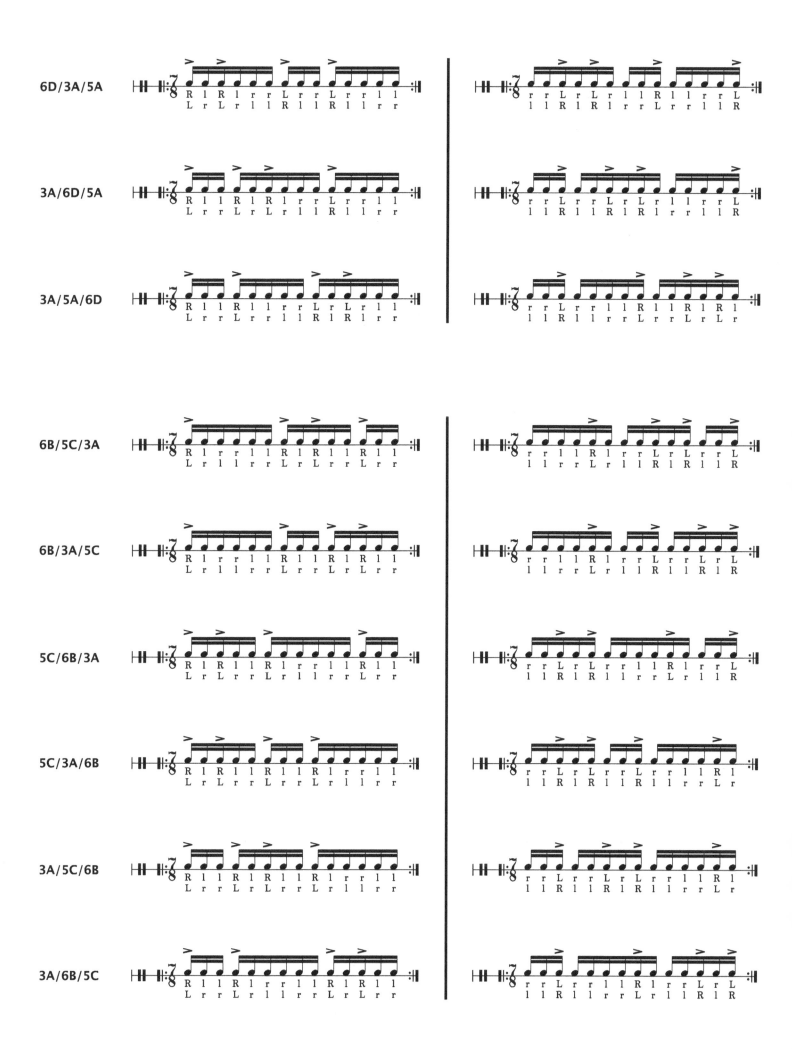

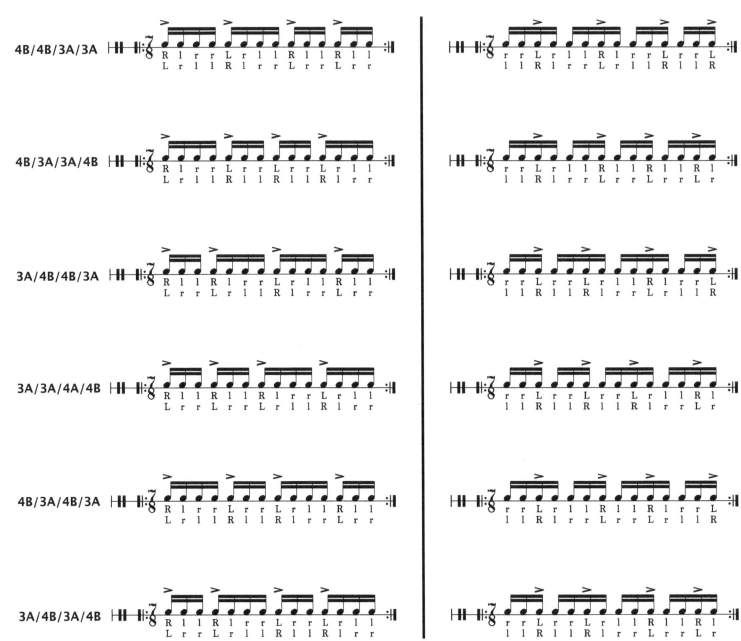

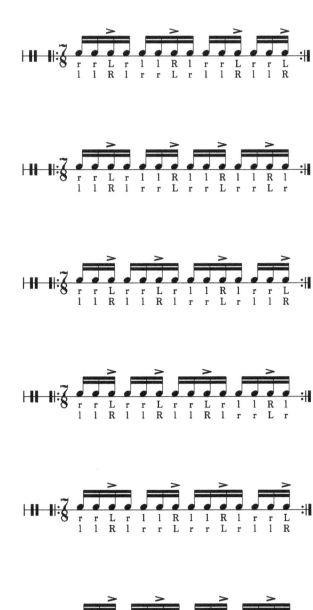

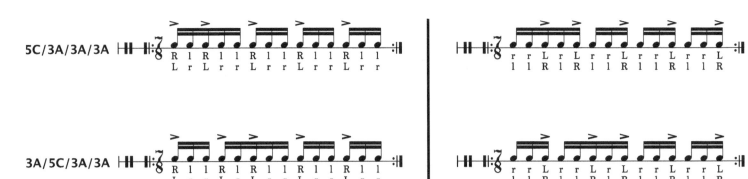

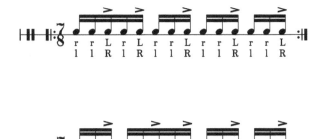

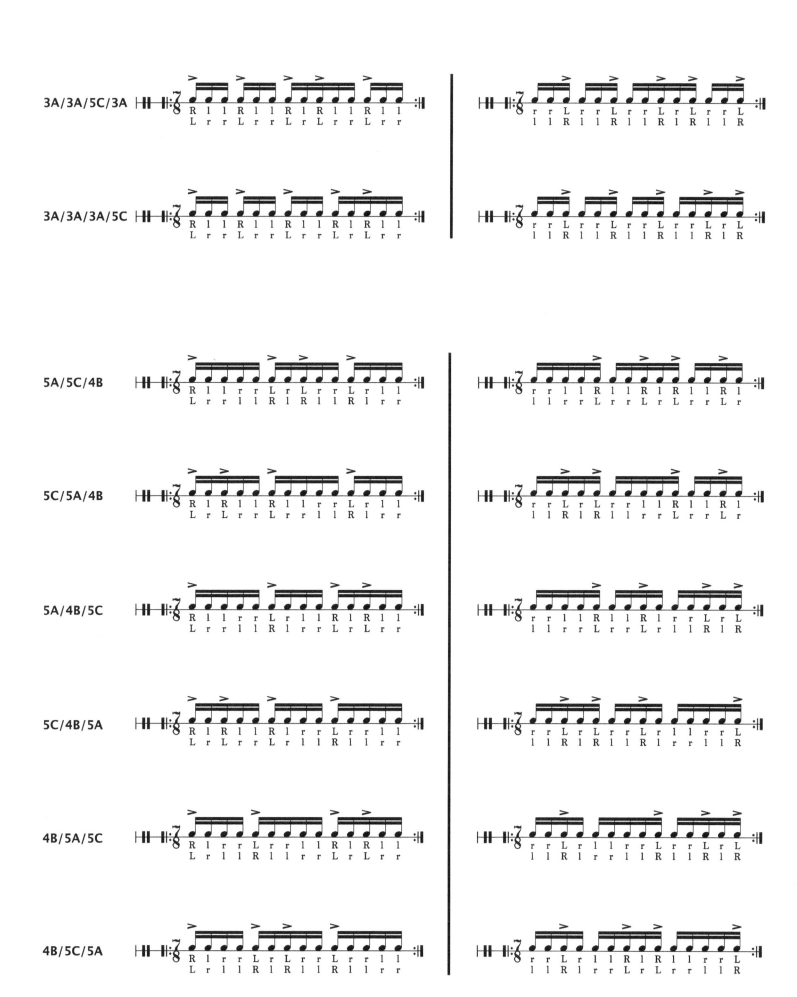

Use this page to write out some original ideas in 7/8.

Sticking Patterns in 15/8

The pulse for 15/8 is:

The notes will be bracketed to help clarify the stickings.

5A/5A/5C

```
R l l r r L r r l l R l R l l
L r r l l R l l r r L r L r r
```

```
r r l l R l l r r L r r L r L
l l r r L r r l l R l l R l R
```

5A/5C/5A

```
R l l r r L r L r r L r r l l
L r r l l R l R l l R l l r r
```

```
r r l l R l l R l R l l r r L
l l r r L r r L r L r r l l R
```

5C/5A/5A

```
R l R l l R l l r r L r r l l
L r L r r L r r l l R l l r r
```

```
r r L r L r r l l R l l r r L
l l R l R l l r r L r r l l R
```

5C/5C/5C

```
R l R l l R l R l l R l R l l
L r L r r L r L r r L r L r r
```

```
r r L r L r r L r L r r L r L
l l R l R l l R l R l l R l R
```

8B/7C

```
R l r r l l r r L r L r r l l
L r l l r r l l R l R l l r r
```

```
r r l l r r L r l l r r L r L
l l r r l l R l r r l l R l R
```

8D/7A

```
R l R l r r l l R l l r r l l
L r L r l l r r L r r l l r r
```

```
r r l l R l R l r r l l r r L
l l r r L r L r l l r r l l R
```

8D/7E

```
R l R l r r l l R l R l R l l
L r L r l l r r L r L r L r r
```

```
r r l l R l R l r r L r L r L
l l r r L r L r l l R l R l R
```

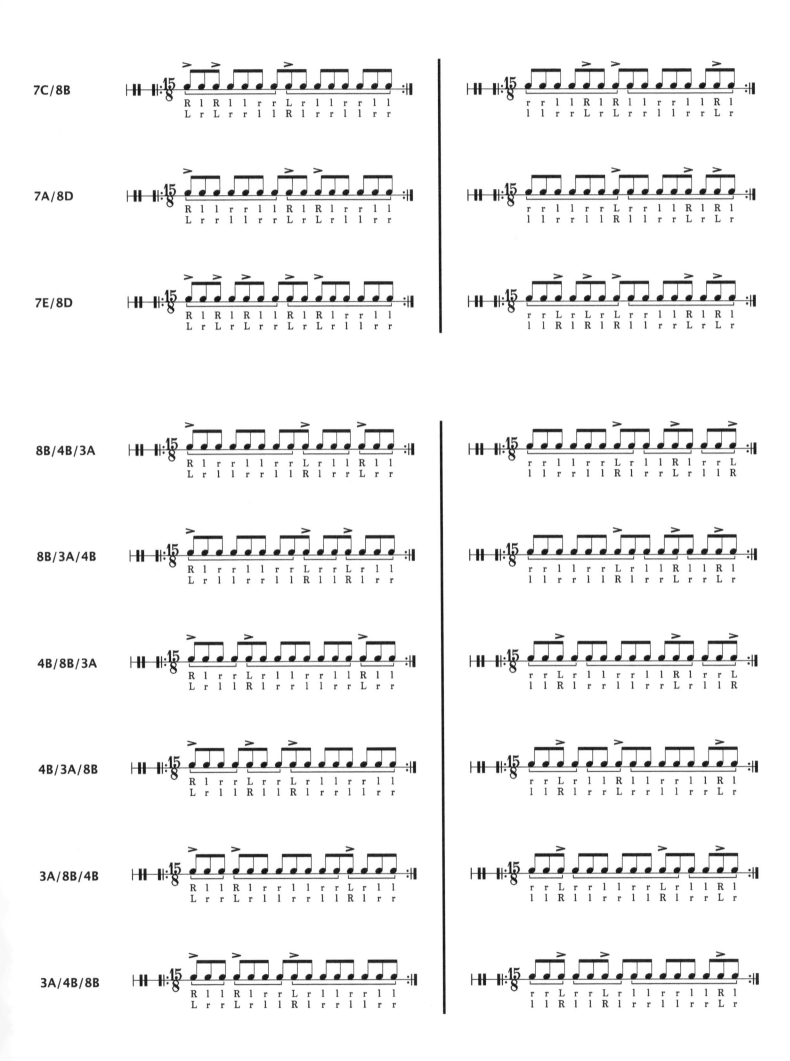

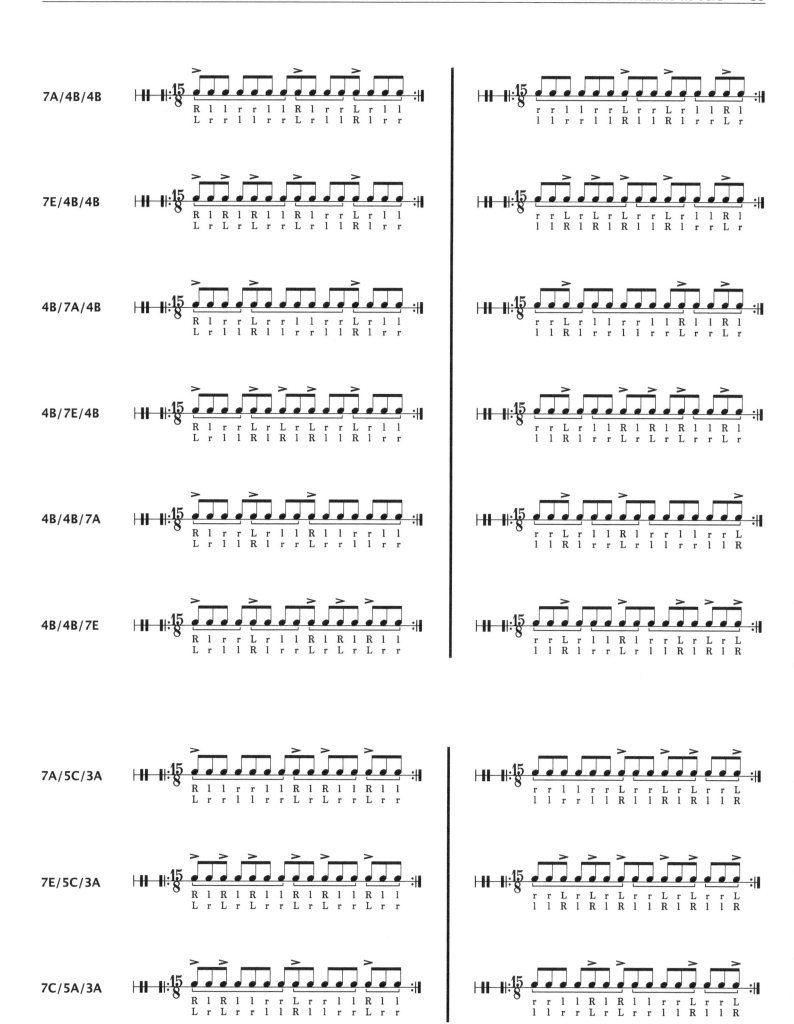

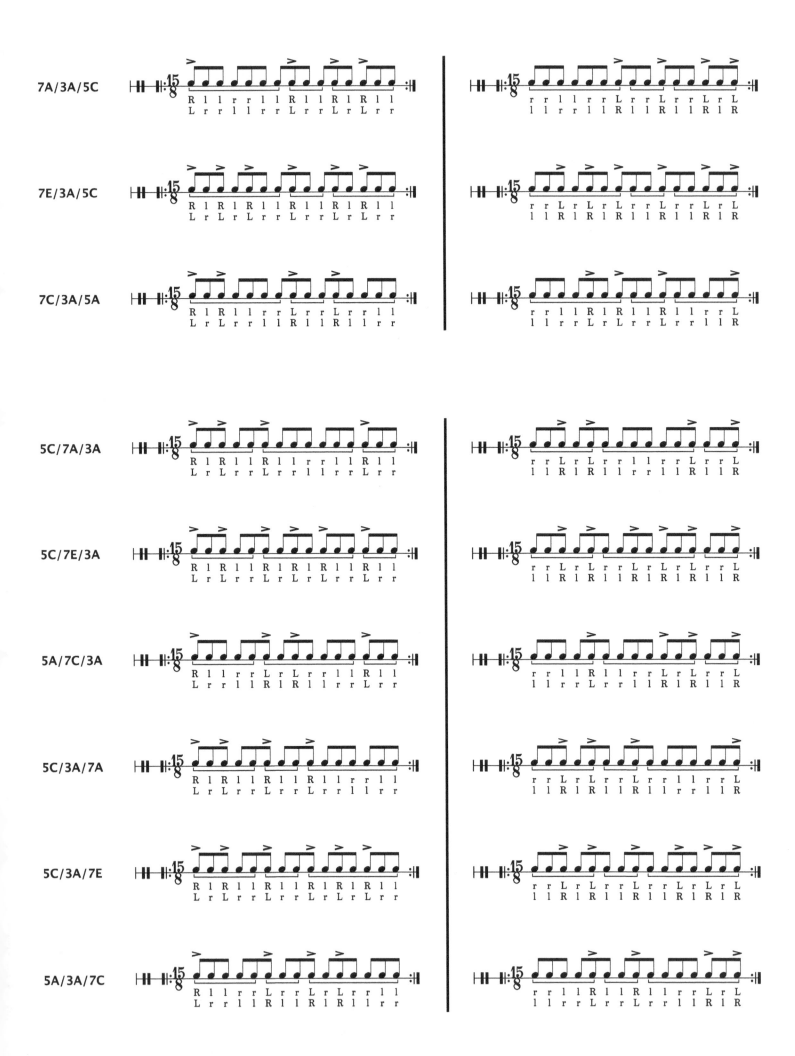

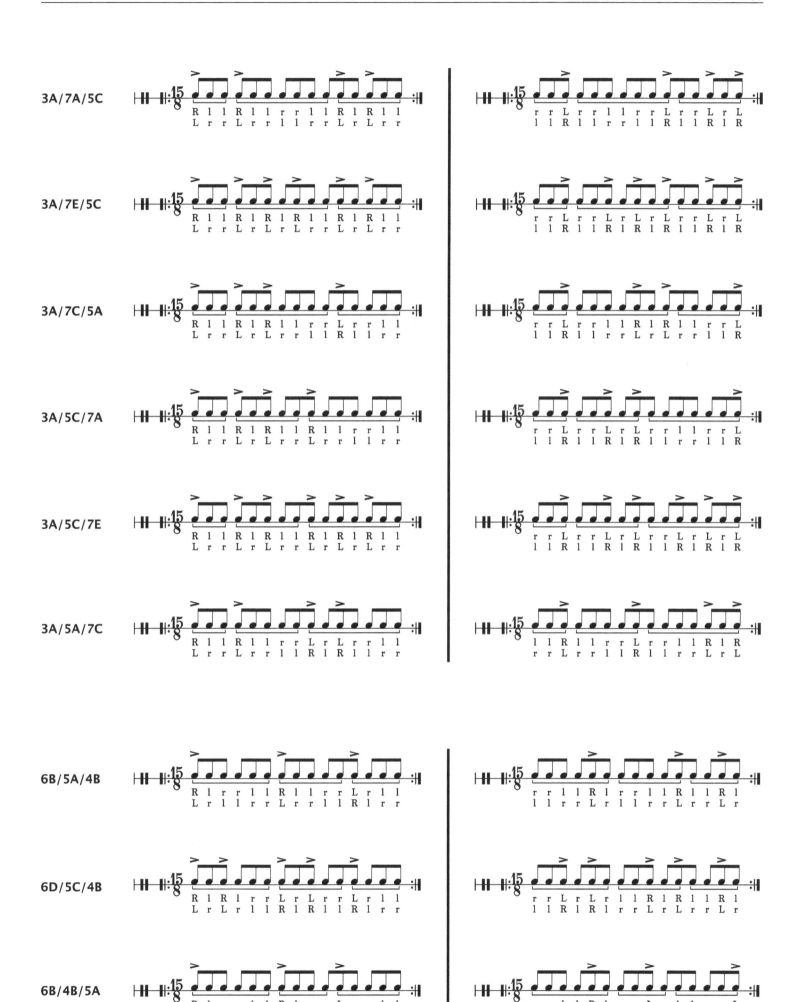

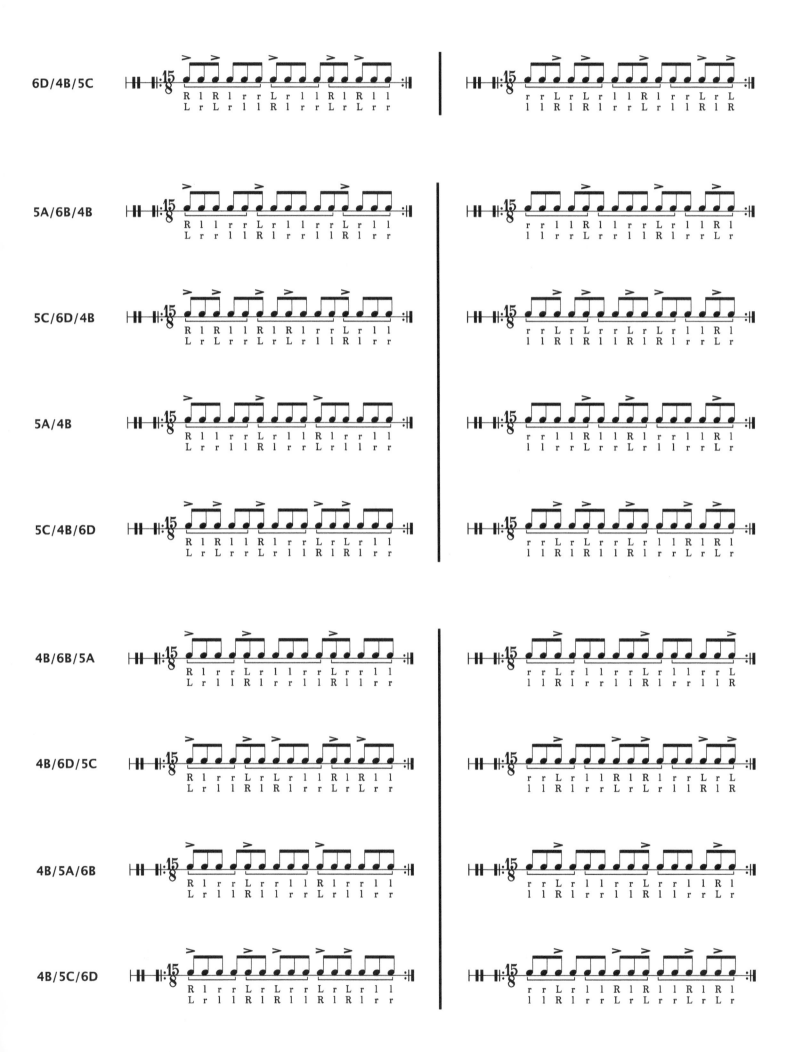

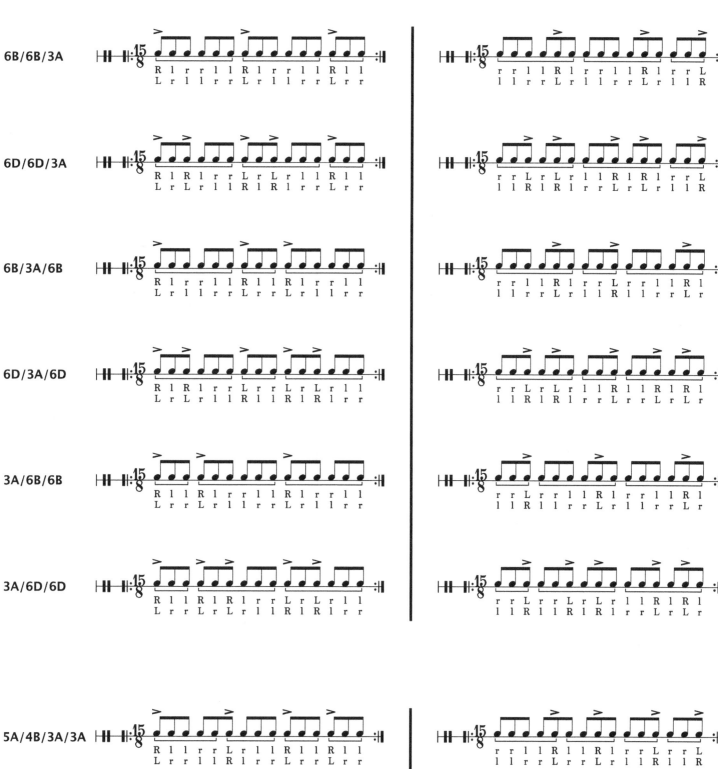

6B/6B/3A

6D/6D/3A

6B/3A/6B

6D/3A/6D

3A/6B/6B

3A/6D/6D

5A/4B/3A/3A

5A/3A/4B/3A

5A/3A/3A/4B

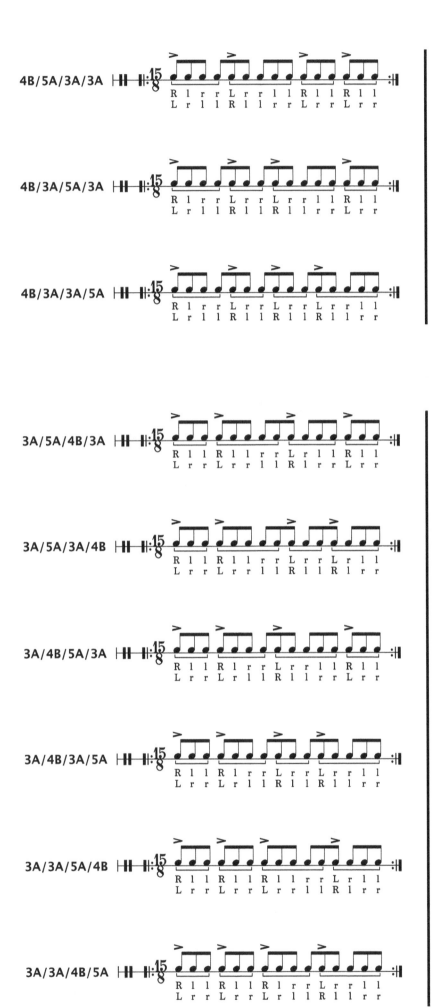
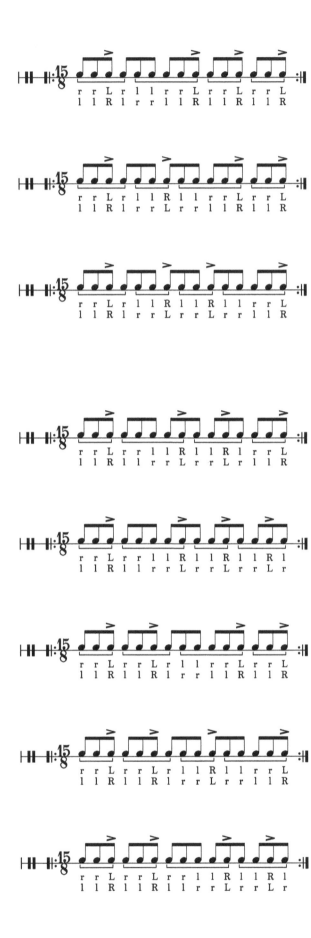

Use this page to write out some original ideas in 15/8.

Use this page to write out some original ideas in 15/8.

Larger Meters—Sticking Phrases in 5/4

LARGER METERS

By now you should be very familiar with the stickings and how they work in different situations. In fact, many of you are now probably just reading the sticking sequences and not even looking at the notes. This is a good thing because it's not really about reading, but rather hearing and feeling the sticking phrases in the meter.

We're now going to look at 5/4, which is a much larger meter. There are over 600 phrases for just this one meter, and so it would take 30+ pages to write them all out. Rather than doing that, I decided to just list them below. You should be able to practice them like the previous examples. Just set up the pulse, play the sticking phrase over the top, listen to it, and then decide what you want to do with it. Remember to play each phrase starting with either hand, leading first with the singles and then with the doubles.

5 PHRASES

5a/5a/5a/5a
5c/5c/5c/5c
5a/5a/5c/5c
5c/5c/5a/5a
5a/5c/5c/5a
5c/5a/5a/5c
5a/5c/5a/5c
5c/5a/5c/5a

7/7/6 PHRASES

7a/7a/6b
7c/7c/6b
7e/7e/6b
7a/7e/6b
7e/7a/6b
7a/7c/6d
7c/7a/6d
7e/7c/6d
7c/7e/6d

7a/6b/7a
7c/6b/7c
7e/6b/7e
7a/6b/7e
7e/6b/7a
7a/6d/7c
7c/6d/7a
7e/6d/7c
7c/6d/7e

6b/7a/7a
6b/7c/7c
6b/7e/7e
6b/7a/7e
6b/7e/7a
6d/7a/7c
6d/7c/7a
6d/7e/7c
6d/7c/7e

7/7/3/3 PHRASES

7a/7a/3a/3a
7c/7c/3a/3a
7e/7e/3a/3a
7a/7e/3a/3a
7e/7a/3a/3a

7a/3a/3a/7a
7c/3a/3a/7c
7e/3a/3a/7e
7a/3a/3a/7e
7e/3a/3a/7a

3a/3a/7a/7a
3a/3a/7c/7c
3a/3a/7e/7e
3a/3a/7a/7e
3a/3a/7e/7a

3a/7a/7a/3a
3a/7c/7c/3a
3a/7e/7e/3a
3a/7a/7e/3a
3a/7e/7a/3a

7a/3a/7a/3a
7c/3a/7c/3a
7e/3a/7e/3a
7a/3a/7e/3a
7e/3a/7a/3a

3a/7a/3a/7a
3a/7c/3a/7c
3a/7e/3a/7e
3a/7a/3a/7e
3a/7e/3a/7a

8/7/5 PHRASES

8b/7a/5a
8b/7e/5a
8b/7c/5c
8d/7a/5c
8d/7e/5c
8d/7c/5a

8b/5a/7a
8b/5a/7e
8b/5c/7c
8d/5c/7a
8d/7e/5c
8d/5a/7c

7a/8b/5a
7e/8b/5a
7c/8b/5c
7a/8d/5c
7e/8d/5c
7c/8d/5a

7a/5a/8b
7e/5a/8b
7c/5c/8b
7a/5c/8d
7e/5c/8d
7c/5a/8d

5a/8b/7a
5a/8b/7e
5c/8b/7c
5c/8d/7a
5c/8d/7e
5a/8d/7c

5a/7a/8b
5a/7e/8b
5c/7c/8b
5c/7a/8d
5c/7e/8d
5a/7c/8d

8/6/6 PHRASES

8b/6d/6b
8b/6b/6d
8d/6b/6b
6b/8b/6d
6d/8b/6b
6b/8d/6b
6b/6d/8b
6d/6b/8b
6b/6b/8d

8/6/3/3 PHRASES

8b/6d/3a/3a
8d/6b/3a/3a
8b/3a/3a/6d
8d/3a/3a/6b
8b/3a/6d/3a
8d/3a/6b/3a

6d/8b/3a/3a
6b/8d/3a/3a
6d/3a/3a/8b
6b/3a/3a/8d
6d/3a/8b/3a
6b/3a/8d/3a

3a/8b/6d/3a
3a/8d/6b/3a
3a/6d/8b/3a
3a/6b/8d/3a

3a/8b/3a/6d
3a/8d/3a/6b
3a/6d/3a/8b
3a/6b/3a/8d

3a/3a/8b/6d
3a/3a/8d/6b
3a/3a/6d/8b
3a/3a/6b/8d

8/3/3/3/3 PHRASES

8d/3a/3a/3a/3a
3a/8d/3a/3a/3a
3a/3a/8d/3a/3a
3a/3a/3a/8d/3a
3a/3a/3a/3a/8d

8/5/4/3 PHRASES

8b/5c/4b/3a
8d/5a/4b/3a
8b/5c/3a/4b
8d/5a/3a/4b

8b/4b/5c/3a
8d/4b/5a/3a
8b/4b/3a/5c
8d/4b/3a/5a

8b/3a/5c/4b
8d/3a/5a/4b
8b/3a/4b/5c
8d/3a/4b/5a

5c/8b/4b/3a
5a/8d/4b/3a
5c/8b/3a/4b
5a/8d/3a/4b

5c/4b/8b/3a
5a/4b/8d/3a
5c/4b/3a/8b
5a/4b/3a/8d

5c/3a/8b/4b
5a/3a/8d/4b
5c/3a/4b/8b
5a/3a/4b/8d

4b/8b/5c/3a
4b/8d/5a/3a
4b/8b/3a/5c
4b/8d/3a/5a

4b/5c/8b/3a
4b/5a/8d/3a
4b/5c/3a/8b
4b/5a/3a/8d

4b/3a/8b/5c
4b/3a/8d/5a
4b/3a/5c/8b
4b/3a/5a/8d

3a/8b/5c/4b
3a/8d/5a/4b
3a/8b/4b/5c
3a/8d/4b/5a

3a/5c/8b/4b
3a/5a/8d/4b
3a/5c/4b/8b
3a/5a/4b/8d

3a/4b/8b/5c
3a/4b/8d/5a
3a/4b/5c/8b
3a/4b/5a/8d

7/6/4/3 PHRASES

7a/6d/4b/3a
7e/6d/4b/3a
7c/6b/4b/3a
7a/6d/3a/4b
7e/6d/3a/4b
7c/6b/3a/4b

7a/4b/6d/3a
7e/4b/6d/3a
7c/4b/6b/3a
7a/4b/3a/6d
7e/4b/3a/6d
7c/4b/3a/6b

7a/3a/6d/4b
7e/3a/6d/4b
7c/3a/6b/4b
7a/3a/4b/6d
7e/3a/4b/6d
7c/3a/4b/6b

6d/7a/4b/3a
6d/7e/4b/3a
6b/7c/4b/3a
6d/7a/3a/4b
6d/7e/3a/4b
6b/7c/3a/4b

6d/4b/7a/3a
6d/4b/7e/3a
6b/4b/7c/3a
6d/4b/3a/7a
6d/4b/3a/7e
6b/4b/3a/7c

6d/3a/7a/4b
6d/3a/7e/4b
6b/3a/7c/4b
6d/3a/4b/7a
6d/3a/4b/7e
6b/3a/4b/7c

4b/7a/6d/3a
4b/7e/6d/3a
4b/7c/6b/3a
4b/7a/3a/6d
4b/7e/3a/6d
4b/7c/3a/6b

4b/6d/7a/3a
4b/6d/7e/3a
4b/6b/7c/3a
4b/6d/3a/7a
4b/6d/3a/7e
4b/6b/3a/7c

4b/3a/7a/6d
4b/3a/7e/6d
4b/3a/7c/6b
4b/3a/6d/7a
4b/3a/6d/7e
4b/3a/6b/7c

3a/7a/6d/4b
3a/7e/6d/4b
3a/7c/6b/4b
3a/7a/4b/6d
3a/7e/4b/6d
3a/7c/4b/6b

3a/6d/7a/4b
3a/6d/7e/4b
3a/6b/7c/4b
3a/6d/4b/7a
3a/6d/4b/7e
3a/6b/4b/7c

3a/4b/7a/6d
3a/4b/7e/6d
3a/4b/7c/6b
3a/4b/6d/7a
3a/4b/6d/7e
3a/4b/6b/7c

7/4/3/3/3 PHRASES

7c/4b/3a/3a/3a
7c/3a/4b/3a/3a
7c/3a/3a/4b/3a
7c/3a/3a/3a/4b

4b/7c/3a/3a/3a
4b/3a/7c/3a/3a
4b/3a/3a/7c/3a
4b/3a/3a/3a/7c

3a/7c/4b/3a/3a
3a/7c/3a/4b/3a
3a/7c/3a/3a/4b

3a/4b/7c/3a/3a
3a/4b/3a/7c/3a
3a/4b/3a/3a/7c

3a/3a/7c/4b/3a
3a/3a/7c/3a/4b
3a/3a/4b/7c/3a
3a/3a/4b/3a/7c
3a/3a/3a/7c/4b
3a/3a/3a/4b/7c

7/5/5/3 PHRASES

7a/5a/5a/3a
7a/5c/5c/3a
7e/5a/5a/3a
7e/5c/5c/3a
7c/5a/5c/3a
7c/5c/5a/3a

7a/5a/3a/5a
7a/5c/3a/5c
7e/5a/3a/5a
7e/5c/3a/5c
7c/5a/3a/5c
7c/5c/3a/5a

7a/3a/5a/5a
7a/3a/5c/5c
7e/3a/5a/5a
7e/3a/5c/5c
7c/3a/5a/5c
7c/3a/5c/5a

5a/7a/5a/3a
5c/7a/5c/3a
5a/7e/5a/3a
5c/7e/5c/3a
5a/7c/5c/3a
5c/7c/5a/3a

5a/5a/7a/3a
5c/5c/7a/3a
5a/5a/7e/3a
5c/5c/7e/3a
5a/5c/7c/3a
5c/5a/7c/3a

5a/5a/3a/7a
5c/5c/3a/7a
5a/5a/3a/7e
5c/5c/3a/7e
5a/5c/3a/7c
5c/5a/3a/7c

3a/7a/5a/5a
3a/7a/5c/5c
3a/7e/5a/5a
3a/7e/5c/5c
3a/7c/5a/5c
3a/7c/5c/5a

3a/5a/7a/5a
3a/5c/7a/5c
3a/5a/7e/5a
3a/5c/7e/5c
3a/5a/7c/5c
3a/5c/7c/5a

3a/5a/5a/7a
3a/5c/5c/7a
3a/5a/5a/7e
3a/5c/5c/7e
3a/5a/5c/7c
3a/5c/5a/7c

7/5/4/4/ PHRASES

7a/5c/4b/4b
7e/5c/4b/4b
7c/5a/4b/4b

7a/4b/5c/4b
7e/4b/5c/4b
7c/4b/5a/4b

7a/4b/4b/5c
7e/4b/4b/5c
7c/4b/4b/5a

5c/7a/4b/4b
5c/7e/4b/4b
5a/7c/4b/4b

5c/4b/7a/4b
5c/4b/7e/4b
5a/4b/7c/4b

5c/4b/4b/7a
5c/4b/4b/7e
5a/4b/4b/7c

4b/7a/5c/4b
4b/7e/5c/4b
4b/7c/5a/4b
4b/7a/4b/5c
4b/7e/4b/5c
4b/7c/4b/5a

4b/5c/7a/4b
4b/5c/7e/4b
4b/5a/7c/4b
4b/5c/4b/7a
4b/5c/4b/7e
4b/5a/4b/7c

4b/4b/7a/5c
4b/4b/7e/5c
4b/4b/7c/5a
4b/4b/5c/7a
4b/4b/5c/7e
4b/4b/5a/7c

6/6/4/4 Phrases

6b/6b/4b/4b
6d/6d/4b/4b
6b/4b/4b/6b
6d/4b/4b/6d
6b/4b/6b/4b
6d/4b/6d/4b

4b/6b/6b/4b
4b/6d/6d/4b
4b/6b/4b/6b
4b/6d/4b/6d
4b/4b/6b/6b
4b/4b/6d/6d

6/6/5/3 Phrases

6b/6b/5c/3a
6d/6d/5c/3a
6b/6d/5a/3a
6d/6b/5a/3a

6b/6b/3a/5c
6d/6d/3a/5c
6b/6d/3a/5a
6d/6b/3a/5a

6b/5c/6b/3a
6d/5c/6d/3a
6b/5a/6d/3a
6d/5a/6b/3a

6b/5c/3a/6b
6d/5c/3a/6d
6b/5a/3a/6d
6d/5a/3a/6b

6b/3a/6b/5c
6d/3a/6d/5c
6b/3a/6d/5a
6d/3a/6b/5a

6b/3a/5c/6b
6d/3a/5c/6d
6b/3a/5a/6d
6d/3a/5a/6b

5c/6b/6b/3a
5c/6d/6d/3a
5a/6b/6d/3a
5a/6d/6b/3a

5c/6b/3a/6b
5c/6d/3a/6d
5a/6b/3a/6d
5a/6d/3a/6b

5c/3a/6b/6b
5c/3a/6d/6d
5a/3a/6b/6d
5a/3a/6d/6b

3a/6b/6b/5c
3a/6d/6d/5c
3a/6b/6d/5a
3a/6d/6b/5a

3a/6b/5c/6b
3a/6d/5c/6d
3a/6b/5a/6d
3a/6d/5a/6b

3a/5c/6b/6b
3a/5c/6d/6d
3a/5a/6b/6d
3a/5a/6d/6b

6/4/4/3/3 Phrases

6b/4b/4b/3a/3a
6b/4b/3a/4b/3a
6b/4b/3a/3a/4b

6b/3a/3a/4b/4b
6b/3a/4b/3a/4b
6b/3a/4b/4b/3a

4b/6b/4b/3a/3a
4b/6b/3a/4b/3a
4b/6b/3a/3a/4b

4b/3a/6b/4b/3a
4b/3a/6b/3a/4b
4b/3a/4b/6b/3a
4b/3a/4b/3a/6b
4b/3a/3a/6b/4b
4b/3a/3a/4b/6b

3a/6b/4b/4b/3a
3a/6b/4b/3a/4b
3a/6b/3a/4b/4b

3a/4b/6b/4b/3a
3a/4b/6b/3a/4b
3a/4b/4b/6b/3a
3a/4b/4b/3a/6b
3a/4b/3a/6b/4b
3a/4b/3a/4b/6b

6/5/3/3/3 PHRASES

6b/5c/3a/3a/3a
6d/5a/3a/3a/3a

6b/3a/5c/3a/3a
6d/3a/5a/3a/3a
6b/3a/3a/5c/3a
6d/3a/3a/5a/3a
6b/3a/3a/3a/5c
6d/3a/3a/3a/5a

5c/6b/3a/3a/3a
5a/6d/3a/3a/3a
5c/3a/6b/3a/3a
5a/3a/6d/3a/3a
5c/3a/3a/6b/3a
5a/3a/3a/6d/3a
5c/3a/3a/3a/6b
5a/3a/3a/3a/6d

3a/6b/5c/3a/3a
3a/6d/5a/3a/3a
3a/6b/3a/5c/3a
3a/6d/3a/5a/3a
3a/6b/3a/3a/5c
3a/6d/3a/3a/5a

3a/5c/6b/3a/3a
3a/5a/6d/3a/3a
3a/5c/3a/6b/3a
3a/5a/3a/6d/3a
3a/5c/3a/3a/6b
3a/5a/3a/3a/6d

3a/3a/6b/5c/3a
3a/3a/6d/5a/3a
3a/3a/6b/3a/5c
3a/3a/6d/3a/5a

3a/3a/5c/6b/3a
3a/3a/5a/6d/3a
3a/3a/5c/3a/6b
3a/3a/5a/3a/6d

3a/3a/3a/6b/5c
3a/3a/3a/6d/5a
3a/3a/3a/5c/6b
3a/3a/3a/5a/6d

6/5/5/4 PHRASES

6b/5a/5c/4b
6b/5c/5a/4b
6d/5c/5c/4b
6d/5a/5a/4b
6b/5a/4b/5c
6b/5c/4b/5a
6d/5a/4b/5a
6d/5c/4b/5c

6b/4b/5c/5a
6b/4b/5a/5c
6d/4b/5a/5a
6d/4b/5c/5c

5a/6b/5c/4b
5c/6b/5a/4b
5a/6d/5a/4b
5c/6b/5a/4b

5a/6b/4b/5c
5c/6b/4b/5a
5a/6d/4b/5a
5c/6d/4b/5c

5a/5c/6b/4b
5c/5a/6b/4b
5c/5c/6d/4b
5a/5a/6d/4b

5a/5c/4b/6b
5c/5a/4b/6b
5a/5a/4b/6d
5c/5c/4b/6d

5a/4b/5c/6b
5c/4b/5a/6b
5a/4b/5a/6d
5c/4b/5c/6d

5a/4b/6b/5c
5c/4b/6b/5a
5a/4b/6d/5a
5c/4b/6d/5c

4b/6b/5a/5c
4b/6b/5c/5a
4b/6d/5a/5a
4b/6d/5c/5c

4b/5a/6b/5c
4b/5c/6b/5a
4b/5a/6d/5a
4b/5c/6d/5c

4b/5a/5c/6b
4b/5c/5a/6b
4b/5a/5a/6d
4b/5c/5c/6d

5/5/4/3/3 PHRASES

5a/5c/4b/3a/3a
5c/5a/4b/3a/3a
5a/5c/3a/4b/3a
5c/5a/3a/4b/3a
5a/5c/3a/3a/4b
5c/5a/3a/3a/4b

5a/4b/5c/3a/3a
5c/4b/5a/3a/3a
5a/4b/3a/5c/3a
5c/4b/3a/5a/3a
5a/4b/3a/3a/5c
5c/4b/3a/3a/5a

4b/5a/5c/3a/3a
4b/5c/5a/3a/3a
4b/5a/3a/5c/3a
4b/5c/3a/5a/3a
4b/5a/3a/3a/5c
4b/5c/3a/3a/5a

5a/3a/5c/4b/3a
5c/3a/5a/4b/3a
5a/3a/5c/3a/4b
5c/3a/5a/3a/4b

5a/3a/4b/5c/3a
5c/3a/4b/5a/3a
5a/3a/4b/3a/5c
5c/3a/4b/3a/5a

5a/3a/3a/5c/4b
5c/3a/3a/5a/4b
5a/3a/3a/4b/5c
5c/3a/3a/4b/5a

3a/5a/5c/4b/3a
3a/5c /5a/4b/3a
3a/5a/5c/3a/4b
3a/5c/5a/4b/3a

3a/5a/4b/5c/3a
3a/5c/4b/5a/3a
3a/5a/4b/3a/5c
3a/5c/4b/3a/5a

3a/5a/3a/5c/4b
3a/5c/3a/5a/4b
3a/5a/3a/4b/5c
3a/5c/3a/4b/5a

4b/3a/5a/5c/3a
4b/3a/5c/5a/3a
4b/3a/5a/3a/5c
4b/3a/5c/3a/5a
4b/3a/3a/5a/5c
4b/3a/3a/5c/5a

3a/4b/5a/5c/3a
3a/4b/5c/5a/3a
3a/4b/5a/3a/5c
3a/4b/5c/3a/5a
3a/4b/3a/5a/5c
3a/4b/3a/5c/5a

3a/3a/5a/5c/4b
3a/3a/5c/5a/4b
3a/3a/5a/4b/5c
3a/3a/5c/4b/5a
3a/3a/4b/5a/5c
3a/3a/4b/5c/5a

5/4/4/4/3 PHRASES

5a/4b/4b/4b/3a
5a/4b/4b/3a/4b
5a/4b/3a/4b/4b
5a/3a/4b/4b/4b

4b/5a/4b/4b/3a
4b/5a/4b/3a/4b
4b/5a/3a/4b/4b

4b/4b/5a/4b/3a
4b/4b/5a/3a/4b
4b/4b/4b/5a/3a
4b/4b/4b/3a/5a
4b/4b/3a/5a/4b
4b/4b/3a/4b/5a

4b/3a/5a/4b/4b
4b/3a/4b/5a/4b
4b/3a/4b/4b/5a

3a/4b/5a/4b/4b
3a/4b/4b/5a/4b
3a/4b/4b/4b/5a

3a/5a/4b/4b/4b

5/3/3/3/3/3 PHRASES

5c/3a/3a/3a/3a/3a
3a/5c/3a/3a/3a/3a
3a/3a/5c/3a/3a/3a
3a/3a/3a/5c/3a/3a
3a/3a/3a/3a/5c/3a
3a/3a/3a/3a/3a/5c

Part II: Additional Possibilities

Through working with the materials contained in this book, you have played literally hundreds of odd-meter phrases. As a result, I hope you feel fairly comfortable with this material. However, there are still a lot of things we need to look at. In the following pages I will be showing you some of the additional possibilities you can incorporate into your playing. In each case, I will explain the options you have. It will be up to you to take these ideas and make them your own.

Alternating Phrases

All of the phrases you've worked on so far have been one measure long. This is because of the stickings that were chosen. However, for each of these there would be multiple alternative versions that would be two measures in length. Let's look at a typical example:

A one-measure 3/4 phrase using the sticking sequence 5C/7E:

Now, here's a two-measure version using 5C/7C:

Here's another version using 5A/7A:

And, another using 5A/7E:

As you can see from the examples above, there are a lot of different possibilities for this 5/7 phrase, and all of them create a phrase that is two measures long. Just think how this is going to expand your phrasing potential!

This process will work for almost every phrase you've practiced so far. The number of choices will vary, but there will always be alternative versions. So, make it a point to start looking at this concept. It's so big you will probably never exhaust all the possibilities, but that's not the point. Just knowing it's there and starting to work with a few examples is probably the best way to approach it.

This will obviously have implications for both time playing and, more especially, soloing. It would allow you to play a mirror idea on your set which could be a very interesting thing to do. You just need to try it out, experiment, and see where it leads you.

Use this space for original ideas.

Combining Phrases

Combining different phrases to create a longer idea is another possibility you have when working with this material. Let's look at some examples.

To begin with, I'm going to take two different examples in 7/8 (7e/7e and 5c/3a/3a/3a). Here's what it would look like:

Here's an example using this phrase as a time feel:

As we've discussed before, there would be a lot of different accent possibilities and bass drum lines available for this example, so just use the above as a starting point.

Now, take the same example and use it for a solo idea. As a format you could use two measures of time, and a two-measure solo. Or, six measures of time, and a two-measure solo.

Follow the same soloing procedures that have been previously described. Remember, the goal is not to find one way to play this example, but many ways.

Use your imagination.

Now what I'm going to do is to take this same idea and rearrange it so it goes across the bar line:

Realize that this process is available anytime you combine two different phrases, so it's definitely something worth checking out.

Use this page to work out some original phrase combinations.

Naturally Longer Phrases

In addition to simply combining two one-measure phrases to create longer ideas, there are literally thousands of possibilities that are naturally longer. Here's an example to get you started:

The meter is in 11/8. The sticking sequence is 7C/5A/5A/5A:

As you already know from the previous material, anytime you setup a sticking sequence like this there are going to be alternative sticking versions. Here are some possibilities:

7A/5A/5C/5A	7E/5A/5A/5C	7C/5C/5C/5A
7A/5A/5A/5C	7E/5A/5C/5A	7C/5C/5A/5C
7A/5C/5C/5C	7E/5C/5A/5A	7C/5A/5A/5A
7A/5C/5A/5A	7E/5C/5C/5C	

Then, of course, there are going to be alternative orderings of the stickings such as the following:

5/7/5/5	5/5/7/5	5/5/5/7

And, each one of these would have the same number of sticking variations as in the previous examples.

Here are a couple of additional examples you might find interesting:

The meter is in 13/16. The basic phrase is 6B/6B/6B/4B/4B.

After working on this basic version, figure out all the alternative sticking versions and orderings of stickings that would work for this phrase.

The meter is in 3/4. The basic phrase is 7A/4B/5A. In this example, the same sticking sequence is repeated three times to set up a four-measure phrase.

There are a lot of possibilities here. Obviously, the longer the sticking phrase, the more choices you're going to have. This is a HUGE area, so just pick a few ideas to start with and see where they lead you.

Use this space for original ideas.

Permutations

Another device we have to create additional phrases is the use of permutations. By taking certain phrases and restarting them from every note, new phrases will be created. As an example, I'll demonstrate using 8D/3A in 11/8.

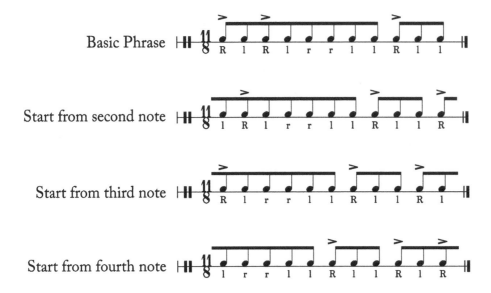

You can continue this process through all eleven notes, which will essentially give you ten new phrases. If you did this with all the phrases you've worked on so far, you would create 1000's upon 1000's of additional phrases. So, this is really big!

Now when you do this, you'll sometimes notice what you create is actually some other phrase you've previously played. For example, when I start the phrase above from the fifth note I get:

This is actually 5A/6D starting with the right double. Just be aware that this will sometimes happen when you use this process. So, try permutating a few phrases just to get an idea of how it works.

Use this page to work out a few phrase permutations.

Mixing Different Rhythms

In all of the previous examples we've used a single-rhythmic rate to create the sticking phrases. However, there are a lot of additional possibilities that would be available if we involved a variety of rhythms. Those of you who have worked on my *Rhythm and Meter Patterns* book will already know how to play these rhythms. If this type of material is new to you, I suggest you look at that book first to develop some basic skills with the performance of various rhythms.

Here's a fairly simple example of mixing a quintuplet rhythm into a sixteenth-note phrase in 7/8. (Sticking sequence is 5A/4B/3A/3A):

You can also shift the placement of the rhythms around. Here's a similar example. (Sticking sequence is 3A/3A/9C):

Another rhythmic possibility would be to use ascending or descending sequences of rhythms, which works especially well for fills and solos. Here's an example in 3/4 using a rhythmic/sticking sequence of 5C/6B/7E. Experiment with different ways of moving this around the set:

Playing fills like this will give a lot of forward momentum to an idea. On the other hand, you could do a descending rhythmic sequence which adds a lot of drama to the ending. Experiment with these types of ideas as well.

Use this space to work out some of your own ideas.

Mixing Different Materials

As if all the previous materials weren't giving you enough to work on, we do have one more thing to consider. There's obviously no law that says when you're using stickings that the entire idea has to be 100% stickings. Mixing in other material will give you a ton of additional choices, so it's something that we really should take a look at.

In terms of time feels, there are really three kinds of materials that are primarily used—cymbal ostinatos, stickings, and linear figures. Most of you are probably very familiar with cymbal ostinatos, as they have historically been the main source of generating time (straight eighth or sixteenth notes being the two most common). Let's look at a couple of examples.

TIME FEELS MIXING STICKINGS INTO A CYMBAL OSTINATO

There are obviously lots of choices like this, so experiment with a variety of possibilities.

TIME FEELS MIXING STICKINGS WITH LINEAR FIGURES

Some years ago I developed a linear system of playing drums. Linear basically means line. You play a sequence of notes between the hands and feet in such a way that nothing hits at the same time. This is really something all drummers have done forever. I didn't make it up. I simply described the process and gave it a structure. My basic system consisted of the following figures:

In my *Time Functioning Patterns* book (pages 40-52), I describe how these figures can be used to set up time feels. You basically combine various figures to create a phrase (just like with the stickings), and then add the accents as well as various embellishments. Here's an example of a 6/5/4 linear phrase in 15/8:

Now, let's look at an example that mixes stickings and linear figures together. When you do this, the linear figures will already contain a bass drum part. It will be up to you to add the bass drum to the stickings:

Mixing these materials together is going to create an endless supply of new ideas you can use in developing your time-playing potential.

Soloing with Stickings and Linear Figures

Just as with time feels, stickings and linear figures can be mixed together in solo and fill situations. Here's an example that uses the five-linear figure in the first measure, followed by the 5C sticking in the second measure. Experiment with playing this phrase in a variety of ways on the set.

Here's another example that mixes stickings and linear figures:

As you work on mixing these materials together, you will gradually get to the point where you don't have to think about what you're using. Rather, you'll simply think of the idea you want, and the material will play itself.

(Note: In addition to the linear material contained in my *Time Functioning Patterns* book, you should also check out my *Linear Time Playing* text which contains alternative linear possibilities.)

Use this space to work out some of your own ideas.

Summary

Upon completing the materials contained in this text, you will have developed a high degree of facility in dealing with odd-meter time signatures. From a soloing standpoint, the skills you've learned will be applicable to all musical styles. In regards to time playing, jazz is obviously a lot different since you don't normally deal with repetitive patterns, and there is much more variety in how you realize the time. For those of you (like myself) who are primarily jazz players, this material should be helpful in gaining more skill in negotiating odd meters. It is up to you to experiment with the various ways in which you incorporate these materials in a jazz style. GOOD LUCK!